A Dorling Kindersley Book

Project Editor Laura Buller
Editor Bridget Hopkinson
Art Editor Earl Neish
Production Catherine Semark
Photography Dave King
Additional photography Pete Gardner

First published in Great Britain in 1992 by
Dorling Kindersley Publishers Limited,
9 Henrietta Street,
London WC2E 8PS

A CIP catalogue record for this book is
available from the British Library

ISBN 0-86318-797-8

Reproduced in Hong Kong by Bright Arts
Printed in Belgium by Proost

MY SCIENCE BOOK OF WEATHER

Written by
Neil Ardley

DK

Dorling Kindersley
London • New York • Stuttgart

What is weather?

Weather is what you see outside your window, from stormy clouds to sunny skies. A meteorologist is the name for a scientist who studies the weather. All types of weather – sunshine, rain, snow, fog, even tornadoes and hurricanes – are made by three ingredients: water, wind, and heat from the Sun. Together, they create the Earth's constantly changing weather.

Wild winds
During a hurricane, the wind blows so strongly that it uproots trees, damages buildings, and causes severe flooding.

Weather watch
With the instruments you make in this book, you can study the weather and predict how it might change.

Tomorrow's weather
Forecasters study weather information, and make maps such as this one to predict the weather.

Seen from space
Satellites in space send back pictures of the Earth that help meteorologists to learn more about weather.

Showing the seasons
Each season brings a change in the weather. As the Earth travels around the Sun, different places face towards or away from the Sun, and they get warmer or colder.

Do not disturb
Some animals, like this dormouse, sleep for the entire winter to escape the cold weather.

Sunbathing
This lizard is cold-blooded. It must bask in hot, sunny weather to warm its body and keep active.

⚠ This sign means **take care**. You should ask an adult to help you with this step of the experiment.

Be a safe scientist
Follow all the instructions and always be careful, especially when using matches and scissors. Never put anything in your mouth or eyes.

Air pressure, humidity, and temperature may change slowly or not at all, so give your instruments enough time to work. Never look directly at the Sun.

Where's the wind?

Air moving from one place to another is called wind. Make a weather vane to point to the direction from which the wind blows. The wind often brings changes in the weather.

You will need:

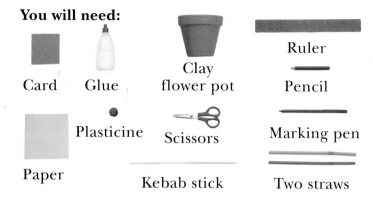

Card Glue Clay flower pot Ruler Pencil

Plasticine Scissors Marking pen

Paper Kebab stick Two straws

1 Cut a triangle from the card. Cut off the top of the triangle.

2 Cut slits in one straw. Push the top of the triangle into one slit, and the base into the other to make an arrow.

3 ⚠ Push the point of the kebab stick through the middle of the straw.

Put the hole in the flower pot over the spot where the two lines cross.

4 Draw two lines between the corners of the paper. Put the pot over the paper. Trace round the outer edge and the inner hole.

5 Cut out the outer circle, then cut across to the inner circle and cut it out. Glue the circle to the base of the pot.

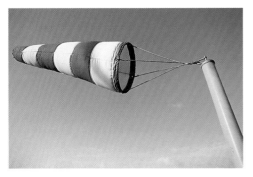

Cut triangles from the scraps of card to make pointers for each line. Use the pen to mark them N, E, S, and W.

The arrow swings around when the flat blade catches the wind.

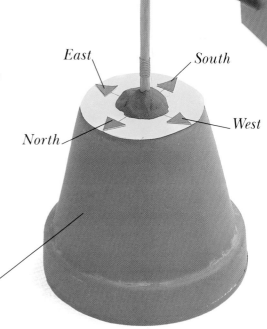

East

South

North

West

6 Put the other straw through the hole in the pot, holding it in place with plasticine. Insert the arrow. This is your weather vane.

Put your weather vane outside with the north triangle pointing north.

Catching the wind
Wind socks are used at airstrips to show pilots the direction of the wind. This helps them to land or take off safely. The force of the wind raises the sock, indicating how strongly the wind blows.

Wind speed

How fast does the air move when the wind blows? Make a wind meter, or "anemometer", to measure the speed of the wind. See how sometimes the wind blows in short but strong "gusts".

You will need:

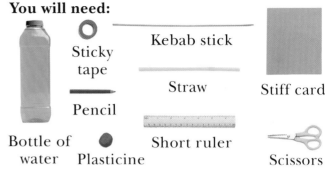

Sticky tape

Kebab stick

Straw

Stiff card

Pencil

Bottle of water   Plasticine

Short ruler

Scissors

Make the curve as large as possible.

1 Hold the ruler at a corner of the card. Hold the pencil at the other end. Swing the ruler to draw a curve on the card.

Keep the spaces between each line the same.

2 Draw lines from the corner of the card to beyond the edge of the curve. Cut it out. This is your scale.

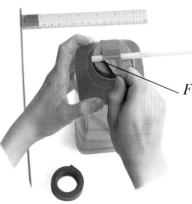

3 Tape the ruler to one end of the kebab stick. Tape the straw to the cap of the bottle.

Fix the straw so that one end is over the edge of the cap.

Fix the scale so that the ruler hangs straight down against its edge.

The speed of the wind depends on differences in "air pressure", or the force of the Earth's atmosphere pushing on things.

4 ⚠ Push the kebab stick through the straw and put a blob of plasticine on the end. Tape the scale to the bottle.

5 This is your wind meter. The stronger – and faster – the wind is blowing, the higher up the scale the ruler swings.

Air moves from areas of high pressure towards areas of low pressure. The greater the difference in pressure, the stronger the wind.

Whirling in the wind

Most weather stations use anemometers like this one. Its cups catch the wind, which makes them spin round. The stronger the wind, the faster the cups spin. The cups are connected to a dial that shows the wind speed.

Sun screen

How hot or cold is the air? Test its temperature with a thermometer. Keep your thermometer in a special screen to protect it from too much sunshine.

You will need:

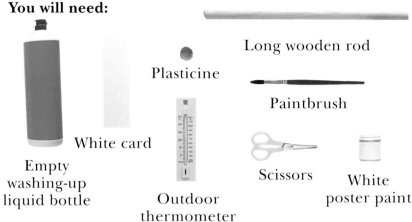

Empty washing-up liquid bottle

White card

Plasticine

Outdoor thermometer

Long wooden rod

Paintbrush

Scissors

White poster paint

1 ⚠️ Ask an adult to cut off both ends of the bottle to make a tube. Cut a hole the same size as the rod in the side.

2 Cut the card to make a shelf as wide and as long as the tube.

3 Push the hole in the tube over the wooden rod and hold it in place with plasticine.

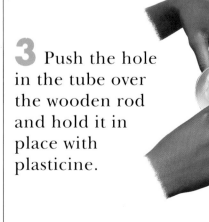

4 Slide the shelf into the tube. Press it down on the plasticine.

5 Paint the outside of the tube with two coats of white poster paint. This is your sun screen.

Let the paint dry between coats.

The white paint "reflects", or bounces away, sunlight. Direct sunlight would warm the thermometer and give too high a reading.

Air flows through the screen around the thermometer, so the air temperature can be measured.

6 ⚠ Ask an adult to help you push the rod into the ground. Put the thermometer on the shelf. Remove it at different times of the day to read the air temperature.

You can also stand the rod in a flower pot filled with soil.

Taking shelter
At weather stations, thermometers and other instruments are protected from direct sunlight inside white boxes like these. Each box has slats in the sides to let air in, and a double roof that helps to keep out the Sun's heat.

Rain, go away

Where does all the water go after it stops raining? It "evaporates", or turns into invisible water vapour that mixes with the air. Watch a puddle disappear, and find out how the weather affects evaporation.

You will need:

Water (optional)

Wax pencil

Plate

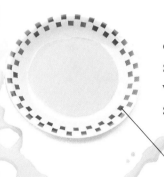

1 Put the plate outside on a flat surface. Let it fill with rain, or pour in some water.

Use an old plate that you do not need anymore.

2 When the rain stops, draw a line around the edge of the water. Leave for one hour.

Daily downpour
It rains nearly every day in this tropical rainforest. This is because the warm air contains so much water vapour.

3 Mark the edge of the water every hour to see how quickly the water evaporates. Try this again in different types of weather.

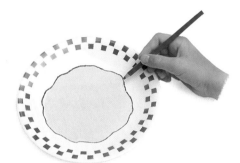

The rain evaporates slowly if the air is moist, and if the weather is cool or calm.

The rain evaporates quickly if the air is dry, and if the weather is warm or windy.

Water cooler

When water evaporates, it takes heat away so that wet things get cold. The amount of cooling depends on whether the air is dry or moist.

You will need:

Thin cloth

Rubber band

Glass of cold water

Thermometer

Warm water

Scissors

1 Use the thermometer to find out the air temperature. Then mix the warm water with the cold until it reaches the same temperature as the air.

2 Cut a square of cloth. Use the rubber band to fix it around the bulb of the thermometer.

3 Dip the cloth-covered bulb into the glass of water.

In dry weather, the cloth gets colder because more water evaporates. In wet weather, there is not much change.

4 Wave the thermometer to and fro. Then read the temperature. How much does it drop, and how cold does the wet cloth get?

Quick chill
Water takes away a lot of heat as it evaporates. That's why you may feel cold after a swim. Your wet skin loses heat as it dries.

Humidity tester

Can you guess if wet weather is on the way? To make a good prediction, you need to find out the "humidity", or the amount of water vapour in the air.

You will need:

Square of card

Blotting paper

Cardboard box

Marking pen

Cocktail stick

Strip of card

Hole punch

Bendy straw

Scissors

Glue

Pin

Plasticine

Punch a hole in the centre of each square.

1 Cut out several squares of blotting paper. Thread them on to the long end of the straw.

2 Use the plasticine to attach the cocktail stick to the other end of the straw. This is your pointer.

Cut two notches in the pivot.

If your finger is too close to the paper, add plasticine to change the balancing point.

3 ⚠ Balance the straw on one finger. Ask an adult to push the pin through the straw at the point where it balances.

4 Fold the square of card to make a pivot. Glue it to one end of the box.

5 Balance the straw on the pivot. Mark a scale on the strip of card and glue it to the box. Mark your starting point with a dot. This is your humidity tester.

6 Put the tester in places with dry air and with damp air. The pointer rises in damp air, and falls in dry air.

In damp air, the blotting paper soaks up water vapour. The paper gets heavier and the pointer rises.

If the air is dry, the paper dries out and gets lighter, so the pointer falls.

Places to test
A kitchen
A steamy bathroom
An attic
A basement
Near a radiator
(Keep your tester away from draughts)

Opening time
Did you know that you can predict the weather with a pine cone? Its scales open up in dry air, when good weather is likely. The scales close up when the air is damp, showing that rain may be on the way.

Mist maker

Mist forms when the water vapour in the air cools and "condenses", changing back into tiny drops of water light enough to float. This is why you can see your breath in cold weather.

You will need:

Ice cubes

Salt

Cake tin with black lining

Spoon

Rolling pin

Tea towel

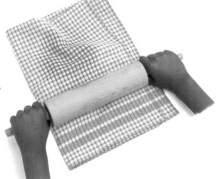

1 Wrap the ice cubes in the tea towel. Use the rolling pin to crush the ice.

The air near the salted ice becomes very cold. The water vapour in your breath condenses in the cold air to form mist.

2 Put the crushed ice cubes in the cake tin. Cover with plenty of salt and stir.

3 Wait a few minutes. Breathe gently over the salted ice. A mist appears!

Misty morning

At night, the ground may get very cold. The water vapour in the air near it condenses and forms a morning mist.

Frosted glass

Frost often covers the ground and trees in cold weather. See how it forms by making frost appear on a glass. It seems to come from nowhere!

You will need:

Cotton bud

Glass

Crushed ice (see page 18)

Salt

Spoon

Petroleum jelly

1 Dip the cotton bud in the petroleum jelly. Use it to paint a star-shaped pattern on the glass.

2 Put the crushed ice in the glass and stir in plenty of salt.

3 Wait a few minutes. A pattern of frost slowly forms on the outside of the glass.

Water vapour in the air around the glass condenses on its cold surface and freezes, forming a thin layer of ice crystals.

Water does not freeze on the petroleum jelly and no frost forms.

Wintry window
Frost can make beautiful patterns on windows. Frost is more likely to form on cold, clear nights, because the temperature drops further when there are no clouds.

Cloud in a bottle

How do clouds form high in the sky? Find out by making a cloud appear in a bottle. A cloud contains billions of tiny drops of water, which condense on to smoke or specks of dust floating in the air.

You will need:

Cold water

Matches

Straw

Scissors

Plasticine

Glass bottle with screw cap

1 ⚠ Ask an adult to make a hole in the bottle cap.

Make sure the seal is tight.

2 Push the straw through the hole and seal with plasticine.

3 Pour a little cold water into the bottle and swirl it around. Then pour it out.

4 ⚠ Ask an adult to light a match. Blow it out, then hold the smoking match in the neck of the bottle so that the smoke goes inside.

Light the match close to the neck of the bottle.

Blowing into the bottle raises the pressure of the air inside.

When you let go of the straw, the air pressure drops and the air becomes cooler.

The water vapour inside the bottle condenses into tiny droplets, which cling on to the particles of smoke to form a cloud.

5 Quickly twist the cap on the bottle and blow into the straw as hard as you can. Stop blowing and pinch the straw, so no air can escape.

6 Let go of the straw. As air rushes out of the bottle, a cloud forms inside.

Snowy summit

Clouds form high up where the air pressure and temperature are lower. Water droplets inside the cloud can freeze into ice crystals, which may fall to the ground as snowflakes.

Rainmaker

Before the billions of water droplets that make up a cloud can fall as rain, they must grow larger and heavier. See what happens inside a cloud to make rain fall.

You will need:

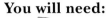

Plasticine

Plant mister filled with water

Baking tray

1 Stand the tray on a table top, supporting it with plasticine.

Small drops of water cling to the tray until they grow as other drops join them.

A large drop of water is heavy enough to run down the tray, taking in more drops on its way.

2 Adjust the mister to give a fine spray. Then start to spray the tray. Some drops of water cling to the tray, but others join together to run down it.

Rainy weather

These grey clouds are so full of water that they block the Sun. Tiny drops of water floating in the cloud clump together into larger drops. This continues until the drops get so big that they begin to fall, and it rains.

Rain of colour

Why does a dazzling arch of colour form when the Sun lights up a shower of rain? Find out by adding some sunshine to a bowl of water.

You will need:

Fish bowl filled with water

Black card

White card

1 Move a table to a sunny place. Put the black card on the table, then put the fish bowl on the card.

As the sunlight passes through the round mass of water, it splits into the colours of the rainbow, which are reflected on to the card.

Brilliant bow

You can see a rainbow in a shower of rain if the Sun is behind you. Each raindrop is a tiny round mass of water that splits sunlight into different colours and reflects them back to you.

2 Place the white card to one side of the fish bowl. Hold it so that the side of the card facing you is shaded. A rainbow appears on the card!

Rain catcher

How much rain falls in a light shower? How much in a heavy downpour? Find out by making a "rain gauge". Rain falls into the top of the gauge and collects in the bottom, where it can be measured.

You will need:

Marbles

Ruler

Plastic bottle

Scissors

Sticky tape

Jug of water

1 ⚠ Ask an adult to cut the top off the bottle. Cut where the width of the bottle is the same as the base.

Make the bottom strip a different colour from the others.

Use the ruler to place the strips 10 mm apart.

2 Stick thin strips of tape on the side of the bottle. These make a scale.

The marbles weigh down the bottle so that it does not tip over.

3 Put the marbles in the bottom of the bottle. Turn the top upside-down and tape it to the bottle.

4 Pour water into the bottle until it reaches the bottom strip on the scale. This is your rain gauge.

Put the rain gauge out in the open, away from trees and roofs.

Record the total rainfall in millimetres each day. Then pour out the rain, and refill the rain gauge to the bottom strip.

5 Put your rain gauge outside before it rains. After the rain stops, see how far up the scale the water reaches.

Recording the rain
This is a rain gauge at a weather station. Its wide top catches the rain, which runs down a narrow tube inside the gauge to be measured. The rainfall is usually recorded every day.

Bottle barometer

Make a barometer to test the air pressure. A sudden drop in air pressure usually brings stormy weather, while a rise in air pressure means good weather is on the way.

You will need:

Pencil

Cotton

Scissors

Paper fastener

Cardboard box

Kebab stick

Sticky tape

Marking pen

Long piece of spaghetti

Flexible plastic bottle with cap

1 Squeeze the air out of the bottle. Twist on the cap so that the bottle stays flat.

Make this hole halfway down the side.

Make these holes near the top.

2 ⚠ Use the pencil to make a small hole in the side of the box, and a hole in each end.

Hold the bottle in place with crushed paper, if necessary.

3 ⚠ Lay the flattened bottle in the box. Then push the kebab stick through the holes.

4 Tie the cotton to the spaghetti. Put the tabs of the paper fastener around the spaghetti and through the hole in the side of the box.

The spaghetti makes a pointer. It should hang level, and move up and down easily.

5 Gently pull the cotton over the kebab stick, and tape it to the flattened bottle.

6 Draw a scale on the box, behind the pointer. Mark your starting point with a dot.

Falling air pressure makes the bottle expand slightly. The cotton goes slack and the pointer drops.

Rising air pressure squeezes the bottle. The dent deepens, pulling on the cotton and raising the pointer.

7 This is your barometer. The pointer moves up as air pressure rises, and down as air pressure falls.

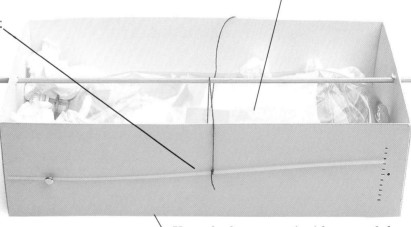

Keep the barometer inside, out of the Sun and away from direct heat.

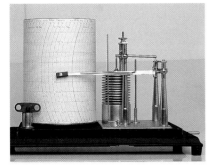

Pointing out the pressure

This barometer has a pointer that moves up and down, showing the air pressure on a chart. It works in the same way as your barometer, but uses a metal drum instead of a bottle.

What a scorcher!

Build a sunshine recorder and track the path of the Sun as it moves across the sky. Your recorder works because the Sun's rays are scorching hot – so take care!

You will need:

Large flower pot

Magnifying glass

Watering can

Aluminium foil

Coloured sticky tape

Two pegs

Scissors

Put the tape about 4 cm from the top edge of the foil.

1 Tear off a wide strip of foil. Cut two strips of tape the same length as the foil strip, and stick them to the foil.

2 Cut off the bottom of the foil.

You may need to tape the magnifying glass in place.

3 Use the pegs to attach the foil strip to the inside of the flower pot.

4 Put the magnifying glass in the spout of the watering can.

5 On a sunny morning, position the can so that a sharp spot of light shines on the top of the tape.

Adjust the magnifying glass from time to time so that the spot of light stays sharp.

The Sun's rays are hot enough to scorch the tape.

10 a.m. 11 a.m.

12 noon

6 A trail of scorch marks forms on the tape as the Sun moves across the sky, showing when the Sun shines and when it is hidden by clouds.

Seeking the Sun
The glass ball in this sunshine recorder focuses sunlight on a card marked with a scale of hours. The heat burns the card and makes a record of the day's sunshine.

When the Sun goes behind the clouds it leaves no mark.

Picture credits
(Picture credits abbreviation key: B=below, C=centre, L=left, R=right, T=top)

FLPA/R P Lawrence: 7CL; Geoscience Features: 25BL; The Hutchison Library: 22BL; The Image Bank/Nicholas Foster: 19BR; The Image Bank/Angelo Lomeo: 21BL; The Image Bank/Terje Rakke: 9BL; National Meteorological Library:

7TL, 13BL, 23C, 29BR; Oxford Scientific Films: 7B; Pictor International: 15BL; Planet Earth/John Lythgoe: 14BL; Tim Ridley: 17BR; Karl Shone: 27BL; Science Photo Library: 6TR; John Woodcock: 6BR; Zefa/Kalt: 18BR; Zefa/Justitz: 11BL

Picture research Clive Webster

Science consultant Jack Challoner

Dorling Kindersley would like to thank Tim Ridley for additional photography; Jenny Vaughan for editorial assistance; Mrs Bradbury, Mr Millington, the staff and children of Allfarthing Junior School, Wandsworth, especially Daniel Armstrong, Nadeen Flower, Matthew Jones, Keisha McLeod, Kate Miller, Claire Moore, Louise Reddy, and Cheryl Smith.